My Brother Job

DELORIS JONES

Copyright @2021 by Deloris Jones

All rights reserved. No part of this book may be reproduced in any form or by any electronic or mechanical means, including information storage and retrieval systems, without permission in writing from the publisher, except by reviewers, who may quote brief passages in a review.

This publication contains the opinions and ideas of its author. It is intended to provide helpful and informative material on the subjects addressed in the publication. The author and publisher specifically disclaim all responsibility for any liability, loss or risk, personal or otherwise, which is incurred as a consequence, directly or indirectly, of the use and application of any of the contents of this book.

WORKBOOK PRESS LLC
187 E Warm Springs Rd,
Suite B285, Las Vegas, NV 89119, USA

Website:	https://workbookpress.com/
Hotline:	1-888-818-4856
Email:	admin@workbookpress.com

Ordering Information:
Quantity sales. Special discounts are available on quantity purchases by corporations, associations, and others. For details, contact the publisher at the address above.

ISBN-13:	978-1-955459-27-3 (Paperback Version)
	978-1-955459-28-0 (Digital Version)

REV. DATE: 23.04.21

I dedicate this book to my husband
Edward W. Jones, Sr.

Table of Contents

1. Introduction 05
2. Job's Conquest 08
3. Eliphaz, Bildad, Zophar, and Elihu 14
4. Friendship in God 18
5. Suffering Prophets 22
6. The Fiery Furnace 27
7. Hurt in the Church 31
8. Satan's Forces 37
9. Spiritual Bondage 38
10. Spiritual Darkness 46
11. Sovereignty of God 49
12. Grace of God 53
13. True Faith 58
14. The Knowledge of God 62
15. Wait on the Lord 66

1
Introduction

This book was written to encourage believers who are facing difficult seasons in their lives. The Old and New Testament Scriptures give a perspective to the meaning of tests through perseverance. The study of the historical and spiritual aspects of Scripture from creation provides a better understanding of what God wants for his people.

Satan, the originator of sin, tempted Eve to eat from the Tree of Knowledge of Good and Evil. Human beings are not free from complication; they are born into a sinful world by an act of sin imputed to them. The environment to which we are exposed creates social and domestic issues of Satan's deceptions. His goal is to make us believe he works in our best interests.

God promised Abram that he would make him the father of many nations and his wife, Sarai, would conceive a child. Sarai, weak in faith, doubted God because she was barren and well passed the normal childbearing age. She devised a plan to have her

Egyptian handmaid Hagar lie with her husband to conceive an heir. God, being a just God, blessed Hagar and her son, Ishmael, although the child was not to be the heir. Sarai's action caused much pain, but God still held to his promise, and Sarai bore a son named Isaac.

When we make blunders in our faith walk, God still is a just God and can make us whole again. Because of God's deep love and compassion, his desire is that no man should perish but have eternal life.

Imperfect faith reveals itself in trying times and causes you to give in to fear and immoral compromise, which endangers the purpose of God. When waiting becomes a chore, due to the progression of time, and causes frustration, what do you do? The answer is to hold on to your faith and keep believing, no matter how it looks or feel.

God tests Abraham again with the sacrificial offering of his son Isaac, but he had a ram in the bush as an offering to let Abraham know that he could be trusted (Genesis 22:1–19).

God opens my eyes to myself and things with which I struggle to obtain wholeness in my spiritual walk. God spoke to me about writing on how to apply the Word to situations, with prayer and supplication. There is something about the power of God's Word that opens our hearts and discerns what is in us (Hebrews 4:12). It works on our very souls and demands that we get in line with his purpose for our lives.

Satan questions the character and devotion of Job, whom God deemed as guiltless and upright. Satan's intent is to hinder God's people and prevent them from effective witness for the kingdom. He is preoccupied with his plan to disturb the mind and heart, with the intent of alienating us from God.

The pain and suffering you endure will not cause you to be utterly destroyed if you hold to the anchor of God. God knows how to send a prophetic word at crucial times to sustain his people. The spoken word from the prophet Isaiah was, "But those who wait on the LORD shall renew their strength; they shall mount up with wings as eagles; they shall run, and not be weary, and they shall walk, and not faint" (Isaiah 40:31).

We bless our brethren and sisters through the spoken Word that came forth from our Lord. He should be a constant in our lives, and we should serve him in the good times as well as the bad times. God prolongs blessings and answers prayer because he is looking for something that will validate our commitment to him by our faith in him alone.

2
Job's Conquest

Job was a servant who walked diligently with God and made sacrificial offerings daily on behalf of his family to assure their right stance with the Lord. He didn't allow prosperity to impair his vision; he operated in humility and was well respected among his brethren. Even after the tragic loss of his family and worldly possessions and being stricken, he continued to respond rightly toward God. "Naked I came from my mother's womb, and naked shall I return there. The LORD gave, and the LORD has taken away; blessed be the name of the LORD" (Job 1:21). Job's wife's anguish caused her to respond negatively: "Do you still hold fast to your integrity? Curse God and die!" (Job 2:9). In spite of the discouragement from his wife, Job cleaved to his integrity and did not give in to Satan's tactics to make him rebel against God. Job knew the consequence of sin and recognized God as Creator of all things.

God allows you to suffer so that you may know him in his fullness. Faced with life's challenges—the cause of afflictions in the body, heartbreak leading to emotional turmoil—you may ask, "Why Lord?" The Enemy plants seeds of discord to cause unwarranted attacks. Family members may come to damage relationships, or coworkers might be cruel without a cause.

How do you heal from spiritual wounds that remain open and infected? The Enemy may try to destroy through pain from wounds, but you must seek healing. After being knocked around, beaten down, and left bruised, the wounds can become inflamed if you do not attend to them.

Spiritual healing is important for growth; it allows the heart to be purified by God so that you may become spiritually healthy and see things as he sees them.

Physical and emotional pain drains the quality of life, and if not treated, it creates permanent damage. It distracts from God's will for you and brings spiritual condemnation that will swallow you up. God's desire for us is to abstain from bitterness and unforgiveness. He looks for positive attitudes in adverse situations. Resist the Enemy of the mind, and ask God for restoration. Walk in obedience by forgetting those things that are behind us (Philippians 3:13).

Many choose to take their physical and emotional problems to the earthly physician, rather than seeking healing from God. As a chosen vessel, the road to eternal life includes suffering, persecution, and attacks. Job was challenged in his body and mind, but his faith in God did not waver. "But He knows the way that I take; When He has tested me, I shall come forth as gold" (Job 23:10).

The psalmist David said that those who have clean hands and pure hearts who do not lift up their souls to falsehood and deceit will receive blessings and be vindicated by God (Psalm 24:4–5). In order to be used effectively, you must release those hidden things to God, who can filter the impurities of the heart.

The psalmist David wrote,
Search me, O God, and know my heart:
Try me and know my anxieties;
And see if there is any wicked way in me,
And lead me in the way everlasting. (Psalm 139:23–24)

The apostle Paul said, "You will be strengthened to comprehend with all the saints what is the breadth and length and height and depth of the love of Christ that surpasses all knowledge that you may be filled with the fullness of God" (Ephesians 3:18–19). He knows about your inner emotions that may be unreachable through the human intellect. God's love for you is immeasurable, without boundaries, and he wants you in his fullness and to have an intimate relationship with him. He is able to pull out and clean up those things that prevents you from a pure heart (Psalm 51:10). Walk with God in his fullness, allowing no separation from his love.

There is a limited time on earth to comprehend and learn about the "mysteries of God" through suffering. In Job's lamentation, "Man who is born of woman is of few days and full of trouble" (Job 14:1). Life is short, and we are confronted with this world full of grief and sorrow. God allowed Job to be emotionally crushed and afflicted so that he might have a deeper understanding of what is within the heart. Suffering is not always a bad thing; it does not always feel good, but it's necessary. God knows the deeper things of the heart and which way it will turn—good or evil.

Job's faith in God did not waver, in spite of his condition, because he had the belief that his Redeemer lives. In the words of Job, "Though he slay me, yet will I trust him" (Job 13:15). Rejoice in your tribulations because you know what you are rejoicing about in your soul. No one will understand the depth of God in your life, the contentment in your heart, or and the reliance on God to bring you out victorious. There are believers who know how to reach God because of their prayer lives and experiences with him.

You are born for a purpose, and only God knows how to prepare. Job went through a series of attacks, one after another, but he accepted his quest in the belief that God would deliver. Job's heart never gave in to Satan's tactics because his mind was fixed, and he believed God. When your life is in God's hand, he will put a hedge of protection around you in the midst of your suffering. No matter how the situation looks, he will not allow Satan to destroy you. You're already victorious and can rejoice and shout now! Those who understand the movement of God praise in their hearts, with the belief that God will perform what he said through his Word.

Prayer!

Lord you know the way I go. I belong to you and you're in control of everything. Lord I suffer for righteousness sake with the knowledge you have a better plan that will benefit me spiritually and naturally. Lord I thank you for your protection; seeking you daily in spite of adversities and setbacks. Lord purify my heart the more that I see things as you see them. Not my will, but your will be done in my life. I love you with an everlasting love and desire to walk and live for you. Lord we know that you will fight for us in the spirit and everything the enemy try to take you will protect. Lord I know you're fighting for me while I sleep surrounded by your angels of protection. Lord I thank you for honoring those prayers I petition I have before you. Lord you said you will give us the key to the kingdom and whatever you bind on earth will be bound in heaven, and whatever you loose on earth will be loosed in heaven. Lord I thank you! Lord I bless you! You're worthy of all praises! Amen.

3
Eliphaz, Bildad, Zophar, and Elihu

It was traditional Jewish custom for friends to visit and moan quietly with their brethren in bereavement. Job's friends believed he had sinned because only the wicked could be in this condition, and the righteous would be blessed. The friends' revelations gave no relief to Job; rather they gave confusion with very little understanding.

Eliphaz, the theologian, rationalized God by misrepresenting him. Through a revelation, Eliphaz emphasized God's judgment of sin, with the belief that Job had hidden sins and was being punished. In this present world, man is quick to judge, not thinking of God's better plan. The Scripture reminds us to "judge not that ye be not judged" (Matthew 7:1).

Bildad's response was the same as Eliphaz's—he did not understand why Job would suffer if he had done no wrong. Bildad thought maybe Job's children had sinned against God. Zophar, the last of Job's friends to speak, had no compassion, which resulted in name-calling and his exhorting himself as a man of wisdom. Zophar was in agreement with Eliphaz and Bildad in believing that Job had sinned. In the second round of discussion, Bildad held to his insistence that Job's suffering resulted from sin.

"For who has known the mind of the LORD? Or who has become His counselor?"(Romans 11:34). No man could comprehend God unless he was guided by his Spirit within him. God is like a well of water from which we can draw and go to be refreshed. The friends didn't seek God on Job's behalf but relied on their own revelations, opinions, and limited understanding what God was doing.

God has a plan for each of us, and the struggles are for his divine purpose. Job's friends didn't understand why he was suffering but relied on their own made up theological opinions and revelations. Job accepted his suffering and loss but needed to know when God was going to vindicate him because his character was being scrutinized.

The final speaker, Elihu, another observer, had more insight than the three friends. Elihu believed that Job displayed a form of self-justification, rather being justified by God, and he needed to repent. Elihu spoke against Job's three friends because they had no answers for Job, yet they declared he had sin.

In his heart, Job believed he was innocent of their accusations, but his failure was in letting God be God. You can't put God in a box, thinking you have everything figured out and what he would do or would not do. He is not creatively trapped by us; we're created by him. "For in him we live and move and have our being" (Acts 17:28).

All things are lawful for me, but not all things are helpful; all things are lawful, but not all things build up (1 Corinthians 10:23). Only through God's love do we receive knowledge to impart to his people. When we are not in tune with the Spirit of God, we tend to develop our own opinions. Be wise in your stewardship, knowing what to say, led by the Spirit of God (Hebrews 5:12). We need guidance and discernment when ministering to God's precious souls so that it may be effectively digested.

Prayer!

Lord as I humbly come before you that I may receive from you. Let me hear from you God. Lord teach me not to be judgmental because you said in your word to judge not. Lord let me not condemn others and be self-righteous. Lord you know where I am in you. God you said in your word that we are blessed when man says all manner of evil against us for your sake. God they don't realize what they say about me they're saying it about you. Lord when they accuse me wrong, they're accusing you. I walk in the righteousness of God. Give me peace and reliance on your word realizing you're going to work it out for my good. Send a word that can be implanted in my heart to sustain me through difficult days. Amen

4
Friendship in God

Job, a man of principles and integrity, with physical and emotional suffering, continued to praise God. Job knew how to comfort himself by praising God in the midst of adversity. This attribute is what all believers in God must obtain to be effective in serving God's people. You may feel alone in your distress, but you're not alone; God is right there by your side. Job was assured of one thing: that his Redeemer lived (Job 19:25). Job felt something on the inside that stirred him in his spirit to know God was there. One of the many benefits to praising God allows you to break through the pain and stress of situations and give you the joy of the Lord that is unspeakable.

Many times when you minister or teach others, you need comforting yourself. Scripture tells us, "Who comforts us in all our affliction, so that we may be able to comfort those who are in any affliction, with the comfort with which we are comforted by God" (2 Corinthians 1:4).

Afflictions will come as a part of your walk in

salvation; they teach perseverance. Our faith is built on the strength and encouragement that God gives when we help others. True intimacy with God seeks righteousness and obedience to do his will.

The hymn that comes to mind was written in 1855 by Joseph M. Scriven.

> What a friend we have in Jesus,
> All our sins and griefs to bear!
> What a privilege to carry
> Everything to God in prayer!
> Oh, what peace we often forfeit,
> Oh, what needless pain we bear,
> All because we do not carry
> Everything to God in prayer!

Delight yourself in the Lord to reach a level of total submission to his will. Be attentive to his voice that you may hear him speak by fasting, praying, and meditating daily, making him your constant companion and building a solid foundation. There comes a yearning to hear more from him and stay with him, just to be in his presence.

Growing in God, your reliance on hearing from him becomes a part of you. Oh! How wonderful it is to be his presence! Scripture tells us, "Oh, taste and see that the LORD is good; Blessed is the man who trusts in Him!" (Psalm 34:8).

In a relationship with God, one can talk about

anything, anytime, and anywhere; he sticks closer than a brother or sister. Nothing is off limits to God; he is a consoler in turbulent times. We need him as our heavenly Father to cast away all our cares and burdens.

"No longer do I call you servants; for a servant does not know what his master is doing; but I have called you friends, for all things that I heard from my Father I have made known to you" (John 15:15). We have a special connection to the Father that is above a servant. We obey him because we love him with a special bond. He listens and hears our cries and pleas. There is no greater love than the love of God that is within us eternally.

Prayer!

Lord I thank you for being that constant companion. In times of pain and suffering, you've been there to comfort me. Lord I thank you for allowing me to pour out my soul to you in the deepest things that others may not understand. You have been a friend that stick closer than a brother or sister. Thank you for answering my prayers! Lord I thank you for lifting up my spirit when needed. God you're real God! Lord I thank you because without a shadow of doubt my redeemer lives! I feel him all in my soul, I feel him moving in my behalf. When it gets tough and rough, I feel your presence. And, He walks with me and He talks with me And He tells me I am His own And the joy we share as we tarry there None other has ever known. The Spirt of the Lord is here! I feel his presence all my soul! Lord I Bless your Name. Lord I Bless you name! You're so worthy to be praise! Amen.

5
Suffering Prophets

The character of a true prophet is that his prediction will come to pass. Jeremiah was set aside as an outcast among Judah after God call him to prophesy. Judah refused to adhere to the message from God through Jeremiah, and they continued to rebel. Jeremiah was a loner who didn't rely on man but trusted God. Beaten, threatened, and thrown in jail, God gave Jeremiah abundant strength for the needs of others. He was called the "weeping prophet" who suffered personal grief and anger with regard to Judah.

God used Jeremiah in a powerful way in spite of adversities and did not allow the Enemy to defeat him. Compelled to let the people know what God had put in him, it was like fire in his bones (Jeremiah 20:9). God revealed what thus said the Lord: "I am the Lord the God of all mankind. Is anything too hard for me?" (Jeremiah 32:27). When you are at the point of giving up, go back again to seek God's face with your innermost being. Remember the words of the prophet: Is anything too hard for God? The messages from God through the great prophet ring out in our hearts and souls daily to encourage believers to hold on.

When you are called by God, there will be obstacles because Satan is busy trying to hinder the birth of the ministry. If there is going to be a mighty movement of God through you, Satan will try to block it. Push through, as a mother in labor, to bring forth life.

God used the prophet Habakkuk as the messenger to Judah, who suffered in exile at the hands of the Babylonians. The prophet petitioned God on how long the people of Judah would be at the hands of the wicked. God had an appointed time for their deliverance from the snares of the Enemy. He instructed the prophet to write the vision that those who believed would move with God. The prophet's strength was renewed. "The LORD God is my strength, and he will make my feet like hinds' feet, and he will make me walk upon high places" (Habakkuk 3:19). The prophet's feet would be like deer feet, able to run in and out of difficult circumstances and unseen danger that the Enemy set for him.

This is the way God wants us go in and out, praising him in the midst of adversity and attacks. The Enemy lays traps before God's people to keep them pushed down and pushed back, but there is hope in God. Be not weary in well doing, because God is in control. In spite of Judah's disobedience, God still had a plan for his people. God is sure and allows us to suffer so that we may see him in his magnificent acts and glory.

The prophet Isaiah, called the "eagle-eye prophet," saw farther down the road through the eyes of God. Isaiah's main purpose was to call Judah back to holiness through the prophecy of the coming Messiah, the Lord Jesus Christ (Isaiah 9:6). The prophet Isaiah admonished the people to walk upright and not be caught up with the evilness of this world. Our relationship with God should be fair, honest, and pure, separated from sin, with obedience and holiness. Isaiah's prophecies against evil ended in his martyr's death. Many warriors were lost on the battlefield because of their willingness to do what God commanded them. Holiness is a suffering way, and there is no easy way out. Those who desire to live godly in Christ Jesus will suffer persecution (2 Timothy 3:12).

The assurance was spoken through the prophet Isaiah.

But now, thus says the LORD, who created you, O Jacob,
And He who formed you, O Israel:
"Fear not, for I have redeemed you;
I have called *you* by your name;
You *are* Mine.
When you pass through the waters, I *will* be with you;
And through the rivers, they shall not overflow you.

When you walk through the fire, you shall not be burned,
Nor shall the flame scorch you." (Isaiah 43:1-2)

God uses great men and women of today to prophesy, thus said the Lord. Mighty men and women of valor step out in faith to do what God said, no matter what consequences they face.

Prayer!

Lord we thank you for the women and men of God you're raising up in this day and time. Those who fear God and have carried the gospel to win souls in holiness. Lord we know you're going to raise an army that will cry loud and spare not. Lord we need worker's in the vineyard who diligently seeking for souls with a pure heart. Lord we thank you for your word that you speak through your chosen servants. To those who persecuted for righteous sake and have suffered that your people may hear from you. Put your protection around them and let the blood of Jesus cover them. Lord we thank you for miracles already that you perform. Amen. Amen.

6
The Fiery Furnace

God has a lot to say about what the Enemy can or cannot do to you. Paul said, "But we have this treasure in earthen vessels, that the excellence of the power may be of God and not of us. We are hard-pressed on every side, yet not crushed; we are perplexed, but not in despair; persecuted, but not forsaken; struck down, but not destroyed" (2 Corinthians 4:7–9). It may look like you are forsaken but not so. Challenged on every side, God is there to hold you up. Looking back on things you faced in life, without a shadow of a doubt, it was God who brought you through. The Enemy knows how to turn up the heat to make situations seem unbearable.

Shadrach, Meshach, and Abednego refused to bow down to King Nebuchadnezzar as a god. They stood their ground, not bowing to any other god than the true and living God. The king became enraged, and the men were thrown into the furnace and the heat turned up seven times hotter. Soldiers in the army of the Lord go through a refining process. They are tried by fire to bring out the impurities to strengthen their faith. Shadrach, Meshach, and Abednego believed in God, no matter what the outcome. King Nebuchadnezzar was astonished when he looked into the furnace to find four men, unbound, walking in the midst of fire, unhurt. There appeared a fourth man that looked like the Son of God. The men were not burned; the smell of smoke was not on them. They had God's protection all around.

God's protection is all around you in times of trouble. Stand for God, and he will stand for you. I remember being distressed. Life was like a roller coaster, and the Enemy thought he had me. I began to pray, pray, pray! I stood on God's Word, not wavering. God dispatched his protection and ministering angels when I was in deepest despair.

The words of the psalmist David came to me.

Yea, though I walk through the valley of the shadow of death,
I will fear no evil;
For You *are* with me;
Your rod and Your staff, they comfort me. (Psalm 23:4)

Shadrach, Meshach, and Abednego didn't bow down to serving other gods. Just as with the Hebrew boys, God wants us to stand our ground, not wavering in him. They had the fear of God in their hearts and not the fear of man. Today, man backs down to the truth of God and goes along with the world system of living. People view the world situation in the natural eye by accepting everything and forgetting the sovereignty of God.

God will continue to maintain his creative order and govern the affairs of this nation. He allows wars and natural disasters to come against his people as warnings of his soon coming. Man is lifted up into his own knowledge, and arrogance allows him to leave the truth of God, as with King Nebuchadnezzar. We will be approached by many doctrines. My advice is to know what you believe and whom you believe. I would not serve a dead god who is not proactive in my life.

Prayer!

Lord I thank you for dispatching your holy angels around me in the time of trouble. I thank you for that shield of protection against the hand of Satan who tries to kill, steal and destroy. When the enemy attempts to take my life, you sent your angels to protect and minister to my soul. Lord I thank you for it! You said through the Prophet Isaiah "no weapon form against will prosper, and every tongue that rise up against me shall be condemned, because this is the heritage of the servant of the Lord and my righteousness is of you Lord. I put no other God before thee because you're the true and living God. You live in my soul and I lift your name up Lord! Although in despair I trust you knowing that you're able to bring me out and I bless you in the name of Jesus. Amen.

7
Hurt in the Church

Most of us, at one time or another, have been hurt in the church. Our pilgrimage seems to be made more complicated than we thought it would be. You give your life to the Lord, thinking everything should be all right with you. You may think, "Wait a minute—I didn't come to God for this," but the response should be "Yes, I came to God, not man."

Jeremiah said, "Thus says the LORD: Cursed is the man who trusts in man and makes flesh his strength, whose heart departs from the LORD" (Jeremiah 17:5). We do not draw strength from that sinful flesh but from the power of the Holy Spirit that builds up the inward man.

Peter outlined our attitude toward persecution: we're to expect the attacks of the Enemy. Scripture reads, "Beloved, think it not strange concerning the fiery trial which is to try you, as though some strange thing happened unto you" (1 Peter 4:12). The time of judgment will begin at the house of God (1 Peter 4:17–19). Those who suffer for righteousness and remain faithful to God will be rewarded.

Many stop attending church because of the insensitivity of the church or because they are sensitive themselves. Our expectations might be too high, or we might have preconceived ideas on how someone should respond to us. Don't run away, thinking it will be better for you at another church. You will meet the same spirit at the front door because it is not about you but God. When you're hurt within the body of Christ, it is harder than dealing with someone who does not know the Lord. You expect things to come from those who lack the wisdom and knowledge.

You must go through to become that perfect gem that God wants you to be. He will see you through the battle if you put on the armor of God, enabling you to stand against the Enemy's tricks and schemes. This part of suffering brings you to maturity in Christ by asking him for wisdom according to the Scripture. Although, you come to the Lord as an adult, you are yet a babe in Christ. Scripture reads, "For the Lord gives us wisdom and from his mouth come knowledge and understanding" (Proverbs 2:6).

None of us has the right to boast about who he is or what his status is in life. No gift is greater than another in the Lord's sight. We are only vessels used by him. Learn to respect others in the rightful place

God has chosen for them to serve. There should be no jealousy or malicious behavior among believers that leads to disunity in the body of Christ. It's a hindrance to believe you're exempt from sin and don't have to answer to anyone for your transgressions. God condemns this spirit, according to the Scripture, "The fear of the LORD is to hate evil; Pride and arrogance and the evil way, and the perverse mouth I hate" (Proverbs 8:13). We're not above reproach in God's eyes and will be judged by our behavior.

Stay in the Word to prevent human frailties that cause an error in judgment. It is through Christ Jesus, who redeems and releases us from the bondage of sin. It is he who directs our paths into all righteousness with a spirit of repentance, in case we do error.

Paul's letters to the Corinthians were great work on church ethics. He emphasized that there should be no division among the brethren, and we should bond together in love. Paul wanted the Corinthian church to recognize that if they didn't have love, they had nothing. Many of our brethren have passed on without feeling the love that God says should be among us. Scripture tells us, "Though I speak with the tongues of men and of angels but have not love, I have become sounding brass or a clanging cymbal. And though I have *the gift* of prophecy, and understand all mysteries and all knowledge, and though I have all faith, so that I could remove mountains, but have not love, I am nothing" (1 Corinthians 13:1–3).

Jesus teaches us how to love our enemies through his Word. In the Sermon on Mount, Jesus gave his disciples nine Scripture lessons in the Beatitudes that begin with "blessed." The lesson teaches us the godly principles to follow and how to be blessed. The response he wants you to have may not seem normal to the world, but we're not of this world. We belong to God.

> Blessed are the poor in spirit,
> For theirs is the kingdom of heaven.
> Blessed are those who mourn,
> For they shall be comforted.
> Blessed are the meek,
> For they shall inherit the earth.
> Blessed are those who hunger and thirst for righteousness,
> For they shall be filled.
> Blessed are the merciful,
> For they shall obtain mercy.
> Blessed are the pure in heart,
> For they shall see God.
> Blessed are the peacemakers,
> For they shall be called sons of God.
> Blessed are those who are persecuted for righteousness' sake,
> For theirs is the kingdom of heaven. (Matthew 5:3-10)

Ask God to give you a forgiving, sweet spirit, no

matter what is said or done to you. Don't allow the Enemy to build a wall that is shown on the outside. God comforts us in our tribulations that we may comfort others who are going through troubles. Live and learn to walk according to the Scripture because we are agents used to spread the gospel.

If there is an anointing on your life, the Enemy will try to bring you down at any expense, but God ...

Prayer!

Lord teach us to love our brothers and sisters in the Lord. Teach us to love and understand their needs because we're workers' together in building the body of Christ. God give us the in site on how to minister to them by meeting a need, a word or prayer. Lord teach us how to encourage, motivate your people to live in a way to honor and reverence you God. Lord we bind the enemy that trying to destroy the integrity of your church. Lord teach us to love our enemies and those who despitefully use us. Those who say all matters of evil against us Lord teach us how to take it and we will make it. Teach us stand on your word and apply it to our test and situation. Lord you told Peter that you would build your church and the gates of hell shall not prevail against it. We need your presence in your church and teach us to be as one. Lord let there be no schism in the body of Christ. Bridle our tongue that we will not speak evil things against our brother or sister. God you told us in your word that love covers a multitude of faults. And Lord we thank you for it in Jesus Name! Amen.

8
Satan's Forces

Remain steadfast in your walk in Christ, not leaning to your own understanding and weakness. Man tends to get in a rut if not spiritual, and his reliance is on the things of this world. Solomon appealed to God for wisdom on how to go in and out among his people. God honored his request, along with riches and power, because of his humility. Solomon's weakness for women eventually caused him to stray, and demonic spirits overtook him, with the displeasure of God. He was influenced by his foreign wives to partake in their worship of false gods.

With enticement by ungodly lifestyles, one loses the commitment to serve God and wanders into the areas that cause hypocrisy. It's not enough to study the Bible and act religious. Isaiah tells us, "Because this people draw near with their mouth and honor me with their lips while their hearts are far from me" (Isaiah 29:13).

Satan's forces will turn the heart away from God to the things of this world, elevating them to the place of idol worship. You can become vulnerable because you were born into a world of sin; you might gravitate toward things that may lead to a destructive path and cause your soul to be in jeopardy. Man begins to look at his personal values, power over others and lust of the flesh—and that becomes more important in his sight than God.

Those who have the heart of God are willing to sacrifice their lives for the church. Job, a family man who honored God, didn't seek to be prosperous. He was faithful and guiltless, with no other motive than to serve God. When you have the love of God in your heart, it will spring forth. The Scripture warns, "Watch ye therefore, and pray always, that ye may be accounted worthy to escape all the things that shall come to pass and to stand before the Son of man" (Luke 21:36). Scripture also tells us, "Blessed is the man who endures temptation; for when he has been approved, he will receive the crown of life which the Lord has promised to those who love Him" (James 1:12).

James talks about the endurance against temptation because we, as believers, love God and want to please him. Do not be entangled or enticed by the Enemy's plan, but hold on to the gospel, not accepting everything simply because it is politically correct.

When we listen to different teachings of the Scripture and various doctrines, we're to be careful not to believe every spirit but to test the spirit to see if it's of God. It is not his desire for us to be led astray by every wind and doctrine. We hold fast to his teaching, given to us through his Word in Scripture.

The Holy Spirit that is within us is a discerner and directs our paths. "Ye are of God, little children and have overcome them: because greater is he that is in you than he that is in the world" (1 John 4:4). When walking in the Spirit of God, you have the power to cast the Enemy down and out.

As believers, our primary objective should be to serve and win souls for Christ. Jesus, in his ascension to heaven, commissioned the church, "Therefore go and make disciples of all nations, baptizing them in the name of the Father and of the Son and of the Holy Spirit" (Matthew 26:19).

Timothy admonishes us to preach the Word! "Be ready, in season and out of season. Convince, rebuke, exhort, with all long-suffering and teaching" (2 Timothy 4:2). You are commissioned to win souls. Be ready at all times to do battle against Satan, who would rather that you believe a lie than the truth.

The apostle Paul responded to the church at Corinth on the ministry and what it really means to be followers of Jesus Christ. He admonishes the church to walk not in deceit but all honesty (2 Corinthians 4:2). Isaiah reminds us of the commitment to God for which God looks in our lives. God appoints us to service and gives us a charge imposed by faith, with confidence that he will perform.

Prayer!

Our Father! Bless the minds of your people that they remain steadfast in you and always abiding in the work of the Lord. Whatever we do for you let us do it with our whole heart. Don't let us be entangle in the things of this world that may lead us away. Give us a mind to delight in things of God and not our own desires. Bless our souls that we walk to please you. When the enemy seek to sift us, shake us Lord. You're the only one that can keep us on the right track. Lord teach us to put on the whole armor and resist the devil. Cast the devil out of the mind. Lord teach us to humbly submit to your will and way. Amen.

9

Spiritual Bondage

The sins of our fathers caused spiritual bondage to pass from one generation to the next generation. Many are reared to believe that certain behavior is correct, even though it is not according to the Word of God. Others have suffered abuse that tormented them and stunted their maturity in Christ; wounds are deeper than they realize because of the severity of the abuses. God is able to loose us from our internal suffering that has been planted by hands of Satan.

A woman who was crippled by a spirit suffered for eighteen years, bent over, and could not straighten up. But Jesus saw her and called her forward and said, "Woman, you are loosed from your infirmity." And he laid his hands on her, and immediately she was made straight, and glorified God (Luke 13:10-13).

God gives us the power to cast out demonic influences through the Holy Spirit. You're not capable of fighting this battle yourself, but the Holy Spirit intercedes for you (Romans 8:26). The struggle is not against flesh and blood but against the authorities, against powers of this dark world, and against the spiritual forces of evil in the heavenly realms (Ephesians 6:12).

We must overcome our obstacles to be effective soul-winners for Christ. You can be saved and still be open to areas of demonic influences. If you are not convicted by the Holy Spirit, you tend to override or ignore transgressions and eventually, they grow into strongholds. It is an open invitation for the Enemy to influence your actions. Scripture tells us, "And do not give the devil a foothold" (Ephesians 4:27) and "resist the devil and he will flee from you" (James 4:7).

You will become a slave to the Enemy, and he will keep you in bondage if you don't allow God to purify you. It does not matter how long you've been in the church; you may have overriding demonic influences that misrepresent God.

To rid yourself of these strongholds, go to the Scripture: "For the weapons of our warfare are not carnal but mighty in God for pulling down strongholds, casting down arguments and every high thing that exalts itself against the knowledge of God, bringing every thought into captivity to the obedience of Christ" (2 Corinthians 10:4–5).

The Enemy's job is to keep you in bondage, but the

battle cry must go forth! We must fight the good fight of faith, using our weapons of warfare and crying out to the Lord. He will hear our cries and set us free!

Prayer!

Lord we realize our weapons against Satan is not carnal. In Jesus name, we plead the blood of Jesus over every soul. Those of who that have been wounded by the hand of the enemy and casted aside; raise them up. God the hurt inflicted on those souls only you can heal. Encourage them, let them know that you are watching over them. Lord push back the hand of Satan to destroy and bind every spirit that is not of you Lord! We bind the spirit of oppression and depression that tries to settle in your people mind. We casted it out in the name Jesus. God we come against every spirit that seek to hinder the work of Lord in Jesus Name. Lord, we plead the blood of Jesus for that soul that trapped in spiritual bondage. Cast out Demonic spirit that come to hinder the growth in you. We come against it in Jesus name. We plead the blood of Jesus against you Satan, Lose your hold on this life! God we bless your name because you worthy of Praise! Bless your Holy Name! Amen.

10
Spiritual Darkness

Life drags man down, and there seems to be no hope when the Enemy begins to work on man's mind. The darkness of Satan tricks man into denying the truth of God, and he begins to lose direction in his spiritual walk. Man becomes blind to the truth of God; doubt enters his heart, and he leaves the place of refuge, drifting into darkness and away from God, risking the chance of being lost. Many have experienced suicidal tendencies, which are the work of the Enemy against the mind. This is a warning to get back on track by seeking the Lord and the things of God.

God can deal with the Enemy of the mind that causes you to alienate yourself from the truth of God. The Scripture tells us, "And they may come to their senses and escape from the snare of the devil after being captured by him to do his will" (2 Timothy 2:26). Without the saving knowledge of Christ, the Enemy captivates the mind, and our souls are in jeopardy.

There is a way that seems right unto man, but leads to death (Proverbs 16:2).

We need to seek the Lord and call on him while he still is near. When you see the Enemy trying to cloud your thinking, and you know this is not of God, begin to reflect. Remember what his Word says about your dilemma and what he will do if you repent and have faith. You don't want the light to go out so that you become spiritually dead. The light may be dim, but God is able to pull you from the Evil One's thoughts and the pit of hell.

The psalmist David admonishes us to cry out to the Lord in time of trouble because he is nearer than we think. When suffering inner turmoil, cry out to the Lord in prayer and supplication, and you will gain inner peace that relieves the pressure. When you become complete in God through his righteousness, you will hear from heaven.

> When the righteous cry for help, the LORD hears
> and delivers them out of all their troubles.
> The LORD is near to the brokenhearted
> and saves the crushed in spirit.
> Many are the afflictions of the righteous,
> but the LORD delivers him out of them all.
> He keeps all his bones;
> not one of them is broken. (Psalm 34:17–20)

Prayer!

Lord don't let us be lead away into spiritual darkness. Lord we call on you, day and night; if there is anything in our hearts that shouldn't be, take it out. Purify our hearts that we may be that light that shine on a hill. Don't let us drift into carnal things that will lead us away from you. Give us a mind to delight in the things of God and not our own desires that we may walk to please you. When the enemy seek to sift us, shake us Lord. Lord we need to hear from you! You're the only one that can keep us on the right track. Stir us Lord in our sleep that we will not rest until we hear from you! Let our minds be focus on you Lord! Crying day and night travailing in prayer. God we need you move this stumbling block out our way. God you able in this situation. God you see! God you see! God you see! Move for us Lord. We don't want to be eternally lost, but we want eternal life. Break down everything that not like you Lord in our lives. We want our light to shine! Lord in the Name of Jesus bind the enemy and cast the devil out of the mind. Lord teach us to humbly submit to your will and way. Amen.

11
Sovereignty of God

God is *omnipotent*—all powerful. He is sovereign and able to do all things within his character. He is a God who does not change or lie, and his power is limitless. God's purpose and promise never changes, but he responds to what is consistent with his Word. "For as the heavens are higher than the earth, so are My ways higher than your ways. And My thoughts than your thoughts" (Isaiah 55:9). The righteousness of God will supersede our own ideas and plans. We are instruments used by God, through whom he can speak to give instruction.

We are living testimonies of God's miracles in this present world. The Enemy sought to literally kill us, but God would not let it be. He stands in the gap for us, and when we're about to be utterly destroyed, he says no. There is authority for his Word to protect and keep us, if we live accordingly. Satan has limitations when it comes to God's people. When traps are set for us, it may not look good, but we must believe God.

Job said, "I know that you can do all things and that no plan of yours can be thwarted" (Job 42:2). God is omniscient—all-knowing. Scripture reads, "Therefore do not be like them. For your Father knows the things you have a need of before you ask Him" (Matthew 6:8). The hairs on our heads are numbered; he knows everything about us (Matthew 10:30). He knew what Job's reaction would be to his hurt and loss. God is aware of your every thought and what you will speak before you speak. He is in control of every situation and has expectations of what is right or wrong. He uses the foolish things of the world to shame the so-called wise, so that man might not boast of himself. The wisdom of God brings unity and does not divide or produce discord among the brethren. Scripture reads, "And we know that all things work together for good to those who love God, to those who are the called according to His purpose" (Romans 8:28). God advances us toward the plan he has for our lives by difficult circumstances to perfect us in his image. I've experienced how God touches the mind of someone who has the intention of speaking or doing evil, but God did not allow it. He warns man of impending danger that may occur if we don't adhere to his Word through obedience. God's knowledge is beyond our own understanding. God is omnipresent and can't be limited by time and space. When under extreme pressure, you may wander as Job did. "Where are you, God?" Job cried out to the Lord, but God didn't answer, although he was there watching him (Job 30:20). He knows what you go through and when you cry out to him in your afflictions. He sees the trauma you endure through the test and is right there in the midst of the situation. God's presence is everywhere; he is only one prayer away. The psalmist David wrote, Where can I go from Your Spirit? Or where can I flee from Your presence? If I ascend into heaven, You are there; If I make my bed in hell, behold, You are there. If I take the wings of the morning, And dwell in the uttermost parts of the sea. (Psalm 139:7–9) God gave spiritual protection to those Israelites who remained faithful in captivity through their difficult times. No matter where you are, you can depend on God if your heart is in the right place. It is never too late or too far to call on him in times of troubles. God is eternal, not limited by time. "I am the Alpha and the Omega says the Lord, God, who is, and who was and who is to come, the Almighty" (Revelation 1:8). He is concerned about our situations, and his Spirit will follow us to the ends of the earth.

Prayer!

God we recognized that you're the God of all things. Lord you sits high and looks low; nothing is out of your control, and if it's your will it will be done. Lord we thank you for standing in the gap for us when the enemy sought to destroy us and our love ones. Lord we know there is nothing the enemy can do us unless you allow it. God you're everything and we can't function without you. God we can't move our little finger and leg without your mercy. It is your mercy that raised us up from ours bed, not ourselves. Lord I thank you for your mercy. God I thank you for opening that shut door and changed hearts. You are the only one that can do it. Lord we bless you name! When enemy tried to kill us on the spot and all, we could say "JESUS". You stop death! When the heart stopped and the doctor did know what to do. You stop death! Lord we thank you! Lord we love you with all our hearts. When things are bad "Bless the Lord" and when things are good "Bless the Lord". Because we know without shadow of doubt you have things in control. Amen.

12
Grace of God

If not for the grace of God, we would deserve death. His mercy and grace give us another chance to humbly submit ourselves before him to restore our souls to the eternal Father. The sinful nature must be crucified through the power of the Holy Spirit. The Devil has no more power over those who have been set free (Galatians 5:24).

God sent his Son in the likeness of sinful flesh to condemn sin in the flesh, that we might be saved (Romans 8:2). Through the Spirit of Jesus Christ, we're set free from the sin and death; for the law was weak through the flesh. Jesus Christ, through the Spirit, did what the law could not do. God, the Creator of all things, brought us light out of darkness through Christ Jesus, who became our advocate to plead our case to the Father. We no longer are slaves to sin but are set free, walking in the newness of life in holiness.

In biblical times, a slave was forced into servitude and owned legally by another. He was driven by his master, regardless of what was good, and clung to what pleased his master. If it is your desire to serve Satan, you will disregard what is in your best interest. Some people struggle with sin of their own accord, not willing to completely yield to God.

Dulous, Greek for bondservant, is used in the New Testament to refer to one who is one willing to give himself up to another's will; someone whose service is used by Christ in advancing his cause. Paul wrote, "I have been crucified with Christ; it is no longer I who live, but Christ lives in me; and the life which I now live in the flesh I live by faith in the Son of God, who loved me and gave Himself for me" (Galatians 2:20). Some come to the Lord with all types of uncleanness and perversions, but God is able to change us from inside out. Nothing is too hard for God to heal. It is the Lord thy God that healeth thee.

If you allow God's Spirit to fill your soul, he will come in and change your heart to walk in the newness. God can change the countenance of man, and the glory of God will overshadow him, and he will no longer be the same. The Scripture reads, "But you shall receive power when the Holy Spirit has come upon you; and you shall be witnesses to Me in Jerusalem, and in all Judea and Samaria, and to the end of the earth" (Acts 1:8). God's power (dunamis) in action brings about miraculous wonders.

Paul, a persecutor of the Christians, had a life-changing experience on the road to Damascus that empowered his ministry when he heard directly from God. God used a man who abused and participated in attacks on his people to bring a change in kingdom-building. Paul's countenance and purpose changed; he was called by God to preach to the Jews, Gentiles, and all who were lost. Paul wrote, no one can condemn you for your past transgressions because the Word of God says, "All of us have become like filthy rags" (Isaiah 64:6). Were it not for the grace of God, not one of us would be anything.

It is the righteousness of God, by faith alone, that keeps us holy. He declares us to be righteous, that we may trust him for salvation, walking with purity in our hearts. Paul died a martyr's death. Through his suffering, his ultimate purpose was that Christ would be magnified by preaching about Jesus to lost souls.

The Scripture reads. "For the grace of God that brings salvation has appeared to all men, teaching us that, denying ungodliness and worldly lusts, we should live soberly, righteously, and godly in the present age, looking for the blessed hope and glorious appearing of our great God and Savior Jesus Christ" (Titus 2:11-14). God changes us from the inside out, teaching wisdom that allows his Spirit to flow with guidance.

God teaches us self-control to promote good spiritual health that elevates the mind and our growth in Christ Jesus. We are no longer slaves to sin but bondservants to Jesus Christ forever. Scripture tells us, "Let this mind be in you which was also in Christ Jesus" (Philippians 2:5). We are the light-bearers, always abiding in the Word of God, working our soul salvation with fear and trembling.

Prayer!

God we recognized that you're the God of all things. Lord you sits high and looks low; nothing is out of your control, and if it's your will it will be done. Lord we thank you for standing in the gap for us when the enemy sought to destroy us and our love ones. Lord we know there is nothing the enemy can do us unless you allow it. God you're everything and we can't function without you. God we can't move our little finger and leg without your mercy. It is your mercy that raised us up from ours bed, not ourselves. Lord I thank you for your mercy. God I thank you for opening that shut door and changed hearts. You are the only one that can do it. Lord we bless you name! When enemy tried to kill us on the spot and all, we could say "JESUS". You stop death! When the heart stopped and the doctor did know what to do. You stop death! Lord we thank you! Lord we love you with all our hearts. When things are bad "Bless the Lord" and when things are good "Bless the Lord". Because we know without shadow of doubt you have things in control. Amen.

13
True Faith

Other than God, no one can deliver us from our troubles. We must have that faith to believe. The Scripture says, "He can make a road in the middle of a wilderness" (Isaiah 43:19). When you can't see your way, he will open a path to lead you into all truths.

Our faith in the One we have not seen brings earthly and heavenly rewards. I remember when I didn't know which way to turn or go, but by the leading of the Holy Spirit, God directed my path. Our faith is tested to mold us into what God would have us be.

True faith is when we stop asking questions and "believe God." We may say, "Lord, you know why I'm going through this rough spot in my life, but I trust you." We serve a living God who will show up for us in life situations when we least expect him. That is the miracle of the God that we serve—he shows up and shows out, as the old saints used to say. Our faith in God is more important than our desire for an explanation of suffering. The Scripture text reads, "And I will restore to you the years that the locust hath eaten, the cankerworm, and the caterpillar, and the palmerworm, my great army which I sent among you" (Joel 2:25). God allowed Satan to attack us, and he knows how to fix the situation.

God choose to heal some of his people and others not, those who suffer afflictions and infirmities. It is the prayer of faith that saves the sick, and the Lord will raise them up if it is his will (James 5:15). God has a long-range purpose for those he chooses not to heal, but believers know all things work for the good of those who have been called according to his purpose. Paul proclaimed that the suffering of the present time cannot be compared to the glory that he shall reveal to us in the world to come. God's grace is sufficient, for our strength is made perfect in weakness, through the power of God that rests on us through the Holy Spirit.

Many are weak in their bodies but strong in the faith that allows God to use them in his strength. Although sick and afflicted, we can be a powerful force through faith to the kingdom of God. I'm overwhelmed to see how God uses people who are suffering and in pain to give a word from the Lord. A sainted mother whom I sat with was diagnosed with Alzheimer's disease. It amazed me how God used her in her weak mental state. She often rambled and talked as if her children were small and gathered around her. Then she would begin to pray under an awesome anointing. I didn't miss that prayer and how God used her, and I felt his presence in the room. He used this sainted mother to minister in prayer, and my soul was filled. God uses whomever he pleases, when he pleases! He is an awesome God!

Cancer patients are able to encourage others in their weak hour. They rejoice in the Spirit, catching on to faith, knowing if God chooses not to heal them on this side that they will be healed on the other side when they see Jesus. Paul said we will be given new bodies, without disease and disabilities, for eternity (1 Corinthians 15:52). God delights in our praises because he made us for his own benefit.

Prayer!

Lord Jesus I thank you for who you are. I Bless your Name! The glorious things you have done because I walk by faith and not by sight. Your ways and thoughts are higher than mine. God we know you are well able to heal conditions where the physician has given up. Lord teach us how to catch on to faith and believe God especially in those situations we don't understand. Lord we question, Why Me? But yet we know all things work for good. I know without a shadow of doubt that you have a plan for every situation I'm dealing with in the days to come. Although afflicted and the word said, "Many are the afflictions of the righteous, but you shall deliver us out of them all". The mountains that seem to be unmovable you will move in your time. Lord I'm willing to wait on you with my whole heart and serve you. I know while you're working on the case, as I speaking you're moving things around for my best interest. And I thank you for it! God I remember your word and you said it will not return void, but it shall accomplish what it said it would. It is well in my soul because I believe God. Amen

14
The Knowledge of God

Job's downfall was his philosophical idea on when and how God should respond on his behalf. God answered Job out of a whirlwind to get his immediate attention when he least expected it. God's concerns were how much knowledge Job had about him and his creations. Job had no answers because he lacked wisdom in understanding all the resources and forces of nature at God's hand. Scripture tells us, "Who has a claim against me that I must pay? Everything under heaven belongs to me" (Job 41:11).

God says through the Scripture that man has no power to stand up against him because he is all powerful. Job and his friends did not recognize the full sovereignty of God and the power he had over man. Satan wants to blindfold us to God's limits and have control over the situation.

The Enemy wants us not to believe God for the petitions that we have before him. Satan's tactics are not a challenge to God, because he is already a defeated foe, and Job had to only believe. God knew about Job's predicament and was right there in the middle of the situation, working it out in his own time. When we have petitions before the Lord, it seems he is not moving fast enough. Satan tries to attack our minds with our own righteous indignation, which causes a feeling of anger or disgust. Our pride hinders us from seeing God's real purpose, which requires him to break up the fallow grounds of the heart that we may sow his righteousness (Hosea 10:12).

Job realized his insufficiency in his human abilities and humbly submitted to God. God reprimanded Job's friends in their efforts to mislead him and gave them an opportunity to repent. Job humbly submitted to God with repentance for his lack of patience in waiting for him. God was aware of the predicament that Job was in because he allowed it to be. We must believe God, with the assurance through Christ Jesus, that he will work it out. God's plan for Job was restoration, not defeat.

Job repented for his omission because he loved God, and he knew God loved him. No matter what the situation looks like, remember the love of God. He gave his only begotten Son that you may have eternal life. God rebuked Job's friend for trying to mislead Job to believe he had sin. They judged Job without knowing God's intention. God wanted Job to trust him with his very existence, not leaning toward his own understanding. God wants us to trust him and to put our lives into his hands. Through the love of God, Job forgave his friends and prayed for them. The suffering Job endured was necessary to receive what God had for him.

We go through financial struggles, possibly losing all our material possessions. Families lose loved ones, which brings a tremendous amount of grief. Children fall into drugs, riotous living, and perverted lifestyles with seemingly no desire to serve God.

Scripture tells us, "I have no greater joy than to hear that my children walk in truth" (3 John 1:4). This is the prayer of believers who have children and family members who have strayed from the truth of the gospel. The Enemy tries to make us doubt that it will ever come to pass. Keep the faith!

God has a way of delivering that wayward mind that seeks worldly desires. All believers know that God can change the situation in a twinkling of his eye. Satan would like us not to believe God and his Word. God gave Job complete restoration of his family and worldly possessions. Don't doubt God; believe he will work out your situation and open doors for you to be blessed.

Prayer!

Lord we know you have the answer to all our problems. God we look to you to open that closed door! Oh God, hear our plea, as we come before you in a time of trouble. Lord we know not what to do and know you have all the answers to our problems. And we thank you right now and we believe it is done. Lose your hold Satan against every blessing and plan that God has for his people. God you know how to work on the behalf of your little ones for their benefits; and when the evil one is trying to hinder your move. We look to you for answers and knowing you see far beyond than we can see. Bless Your Name! You worthy to praise! We praise you in the morning, noonday and night and we thank you for moving in our behalf. In Jesus Name, we pray, Amen

15
Wait on the Lord

Wait on the LORD; Be of good courage, And He shall strengthen your heart; Wait, I say, on the LORD!—Psalm 27:14

God is looking for hearts that are pure and willing to wait on him in trying times. Waiting God builds a relationship that transforms your character into his will. He reminds us of the Word; after we have suffered for a while he will restore us and make us strong, steadfast, and unmovable (1 Peter 5:10). God be the glory, from all whom blessings flow, because his promises are true.

The psalmist said, "Many are the afflictions of the righteous, But the LORD delivers him out of them all" (Psalm 34:19). Perseverance in the midst of a test cooperates with God's plan for your life and the benefit of others. Be busy about God's work that is assigned to your hands while waiting on the Lord to answer. Praise in your heart, while working busily for God, elevates your mind to walk through whatever the Enemy is trying to do in your life.

Lie before him, and let him restore your soul to relieve the weariness of your mind. Learn to rest in him with your mind and soul. The psalmist David said,

> My soul, wait silently for God alone,
> For my expectation is from Him.
> He only is my rock and my salvation;
> *He* is my defense;
> I shall not be moved. (Psalm 62:5–6)

Job's dilemma is what we face in our walk with the Lord. It seems that our prayers are not answered, and we grow weary, which allows the Enemy to bring in a spirit of fear. God wants us not to fear because when fear comes into our hearts it hinders and delays God's plan.

The prophet Habakkuk said, "For the vision is yet for an appointed time, but in the end it will speak, and it will not lie. Though it tarries, wait for it; because it will surely come, It will not tarry" (Habakkuk 2:3).

Remember that God is sitting on his throne, looking down at us and what we're going through. He sees the turmoil, pain, and suffering that we are willing to endure, because we love him and want to receive his promises.

Prayer!

Lord I Bless your name! I praise you name because you save a wretch like me. I thank you for the privileges to serve you, master. Bless your name, Bless your name, Oh how I love you. Even through bad times I love you because you been so kind, merciful and longsuffering. Lord teach us to go thru and not be weary and wait on you. Even when I did respond as I shouldn't you pick me up and settle me on solid ground. Thank Jesus! Thank Jesus! Thank Jesus! Amen.

16
Testimonies

Testimonies of God's goodness help others to overcome. It is the reason why we go through things; it is not for us but for others. How wonderful is my Lord! It is my praise time. Thank you, Jesus! Thank you, Jesus! I know him as a healer and deliverer. We're tested in the "furnace of affliction" to refine us, but God gives us the strength to endure. The heat may be turned up, but we can rejoice, knowing that God will bring us out.

I was rushed to the hospital, and after a being examined, I was diagnosed with acute pancreatitis. A gallstone passed and landed on my pancreas, which caused infection in my body. I was placed on a ventilator to help with breathing and to stop the spread of infection. The condition caused physical discomfort and mental torment, and I became weak, depressed, and uncomfortable due to a previous surgery six weeks earlier.

My prayer-warrior friends—we watch over each

other like sisters—came by and prayed for me. The saints prayed for me at church, and there's nothing like people of God to get a prayer through to God.

When my condition stabilized, surgery was performed on my pancreas to remove the gallstones and preventing the onset of early stage diabetes. I recovered and was dismissed from the hospital, but the pain I experienced before the surgery returned. I was rushed back to the hospital, and the reexamination showed I had scar tissue. The doctor instructed me to be careful with what I ate, and if the pain continued, they would have to perform another surgery.

At this point, I was fed up with the Devil, and I always have been a warrior. I took my Bible and prayer to the table, and God healed my body. Not until I turned to God did I get relief from my pain and suffering. I make no restrictions on my diet, eating whatever I want in moderation.

I never returned to the emergency room with the complaint again for that condition. This was a test of my faith, to realize I had to trust God or allow the Enemy to make me believe I would not be healed.

Satan tried to take me out on another occasion, but God had a better plan. I was in a car accident in which I almost lost my life. At a stop sign at an intersection, a school bus on the other side of the street hit a piece of ice. The bus swerved, and the back of the bus, where the gas tank was located, entered the front windshield of my car. I saw the bus coming, and the only thing I thought to say was "Jesus," and I lay my head down on the passenger side of the car. The bus came straight through the windshield, and if I had been sitting up, my head would have been severed. The accident caused a six-car pile-up and left me with thirty-two stitches in my face, as well as other injuries.

Some young men who witnessed the accident pulled me out of the car before the jaws-of-life equipment arrived, fearing a gas tank explosion. As I lay in the hospital, a woman who witnessed the accident came in and spoke to me.

I don't know who she was or how she got back to see me, but she told me that God was with me and that he had a plan for my life. Then she left the room. I didn't get her name, and I never saw her again.

God warns us of things to come and prepares us. For many years my mother, who lived in Memphis, suffered from high blood pressure and a heart condition. I was living in New York at the time, and I would wake up from a sound sleep because the Lord would speak to me through the Spirit, telling me to get on my knees and pray. God didn't show me what was happening, but I just couldn't stop praying a continuous prayer from my soul. One night I got a call from a family member that my mother had been rushed to the hospital; they thought she might have had a heart attack. I arrived at the Memphis hospital in less than twenty-four hours. My mother was in a semi-comatose state. The doctors informed me she had a brain aneurysm and that she'd had a heart attack and possible a stroke. The doctors gave me all the answers they could, but it was not a good prognosis.

But God had the last say in the matter. I left my husband at the hospital and went to my mother's house to care for my grandparents, who lived with her. I went into my mother's kitchen and the Spirit of the Lord spoke to me and said, "Pray." I gathered the family together, and we began to pray and call on the Lord.

My husband came home from the hospital and went to bed. The doctors had told him to go home and prepare the family because they didn't think my mother would make it through the night.

I went to hospital the next day and found that God had turned her condition around; she began to improve. I met with the doctors, who informed me that if she continued to improve, they would perform the surgery on her brain. They gave me little hope for recovery and said that she possibly would be paralyzed, be in a vegetative state, or might not make it through the surgery.

God gave me peace because I knew without a

shadow of doubt that he had answered prayer. My mother came through the surgery with no paralysis or brain damage. She lived for twenty-two years after that and took care of her parents until their demise. She lived way beyond the expectations of man because of the work that God assigned to her.

Prayer!

Lord I thank you for the victory! What the enemy meant for evil, you meant it for my good. Thank you for your healing and deliverance. We know the prayer of righteous the sick shall be raised. God I know you see further than we do concern us. You know why we go the way we go. I know it is for the good for those who love the Lord. And we thank you for it! We bless you Lord! We praise you giving you the glory! Amen

Prayer!

Holy Father! I thank you for this day that you have made. Lord we bless you for mercy and grace, power to cleanse us from all our sins. Lord we repent before you for those things we did in disobedience and sinned against you. Lord we lift your name because you're worthy and we thank you for your goodness when we're not deserving. Our sisters and brothers who suffer for your namesake; protect them and cover them with your blood. Those who are on the foreign fields who risk infectious diseases and danger watch over them. They're doing the work that you commission "Go and make disciples of all the nations, baptizing them in the name of the Father and of the Son and of the Holy Spirit". You know the road that you have us to go and why. We bless you Lord! We bless you with hands lifted up we give you the praise! Lord you are worthy God! God in the Name Jesus brings peace to this Nation. Wars rumor of wars, you said it would be, have mercy on those souls that are being sacrificed over evil works of Satan. Cast Satan out of the minds of these world leaders who do not believe in the Living God. You commissioned us to go after souls for righteousness sake knowing in the end there is a great reward. We lift our hands! We Praise You! We magnify you! God I thank you for who you are and whom you made within me. I know my suffering not in vain if I live for you. We need your touch every hour of the day.

Although we suffer as Job not understanding why we go this way, but yet we believe God. Bye and bye, when the morning comes when the Saints of God are gather home we'll tell the story how we've overcome, for we'll understand better bye and bye. Lord fill us the more with the Holy Spirit that we may go forth in power! Raise young people who can be a witness to what God can do. Bring them out of this wayward generation to win souls. In the Name of Jesus rebuke any form of activity that is against God. Bring them out! Loose your hold Satan! In the Names, Jesus cast the Satan out of the mind! God raise up true warrior that have the mind of a Christ who willing to suffer for souls. Send warriors who willing to step up and say "No More Devil". Lord I bless you! I Praise You in Jesus Name. Amen.

Index to Scripture References

I Corinthians 10:23...16

I Corinthians 13:1-3..33

I Corinthians 15:52...60

I John 4:4..39

I Peter 4:12..31

I Peter 4: 17-19..32

I Peter 5:10..66

2 Corinthians 1:4..18

2 Corinthian 4:2...38

2 Corinthians 4:7-9..27

2 Corinthian 10:4-5..43

2 Timothy 2:26..46

2 Timothy 3:12..24

2 Timothy 4:2..39

3 John 1:4..64

Acts 1:8..54

Acts 17:28..16

Ephesians 3: 18-19...10

Ephesians 4:27...43

Ephesians 6:12..43
Galatians 2:20..54
Galatians 5:24..53
Habakkuk 2:3..67
Habakkuk 3:19..23
Hebrews 5:12..16
Hosea 10:12..63
Isaiah 9:6..24
Isaiah 29:13..37
Isaiah 43:1-2..25
Isaiah 43:19..58
Isaiah 55:9..49
Isaiah 64:6..55
James 1:12..38
James 4:7..43
James 5:15..59
Jeremiah 17:5..31
Jeremiah 20:9..22
Jeremiah 32:27..22
Job 1:21..8
Job 2:9..8
Job 13:15..11

Job 14:1	11
Job 19:25	18
Job 23:10	10
Job 30:20	51
Job 41:11	62
Job 42:2	50
Joel 2:25	59
John 15:15	20
Luke 13: 10-13	42
Luke 21:36	38
Matthew 5:3-10	34
Matthew 6:8	50
Matthew 7:1	14
Matthew 10:30	50
Matthew 26:19	39
Philippians 2:5	56
Philippians 3:13	9
Proverbs 2:6	32
Proverbs 8:13	33
Proverbs 16:2	47
Psalm 23:4	28
Psalm 24:4-5	10

Psalm 27:14	66
Psalm 34:8	19
Psalm 34:19	66
Psalm 34:17-20	47
Psalm 51:10	10
Psalm 62:5-6	67
Psalm 139:7-9	51
Psalm 139: 23-24	10
Revelation 1:8	51
Romans 8:2	53
Romans 8:26	43
Romans 8:28	50
Romans 11:34	15
Titus 2: 11-14	55